T0149392

The Dream Collection

A SELECTION OF POEMS

Sylvia Pandit

 iUniverse®

THE DREAM COLLECTION
A SELECTION OF POEMS

iUniverse books may be ordered through booksellers or by contacting:

iUniverse
1663 Liberty Drive
Bloomington, IN 47403
www.iuniverse.com
1-800-Authors (1-800-288-4677)

ISBN: 978-1-5320-8911-4 (sc)
ISBN: 978-1-5320-8912-1 (e)

Print information available on the last page.

iUniverse rev. date: 11/21/2019

Contents

Dedicated to dreamers everywhere

The Mountain and the Cloud

One day Princess Cloud
Was requesting the mountain,
Oh dear Mountain could you please
Let me rest on your chest?

I am tired dear Mountain!
For a long time I have been
Moving here and there
Now I want to rest
Would you please give me space
On your chest?

Listening to Princess Cloud
Mountain became happy
Then he offered the Princess
I will give you space
If I get you forever in my chest

Listening to the offer of the Mountain,
Princess Cloud got hurt,
In reply she said,
If I would be yours,
Do you have any idea of
What would happen
To the world?
Who would pour the water
In to the world?

If the world would not get water,
the land would be dry,
Humans would be in trouble,
The nature would be lost,
Nothing would remain
Then what would happen?

No one would visit you
To enjoy your beauty,
No one would look at you
To feel your stature,
I would never come to you
To share my experience.

Please don't love me
Dear Mountain.
No one can separate us,
If we would be just friends.
If you stay on the chest of
The world and
If I play in the blue sky

In the lift

I was watching them,
Staying inside the lift.
They were two,
A boy and a girl,
I was in between them.

They were doing nothing,
But staring and smiling.
The girl was looking bubbly,
And the boy was nervous.
I saw him looking at the girl,
Without blinking.

I was busy texting my friend,
Was trying to ignore them,
But failed.
I heard the boy was saying
"You are so beautiful"
Listening to the boy,
The girl was laughing endlessly
touching his forehead with love
saying nothing, but smiling.

I was with them,
They were two.
I was in between them
Sometime life is so beautiful
Does not matter you are
with who!

Avoid

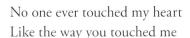

No one ever touched my heart
Like the way you touched me

No one ever help me dreaming
Like the way you did me

I am helpless can't avoid you
Could you please guide me
What to do?

Fighting myself to stay away
Could you please suggest me
how to do that in a decent way?

I love you and can't stop
Myself loving you
I see you everywhere
Sometime inside my heart
Sometime in the open sky
Please don't go away
And never say good bye

Be smart

Have you ever think
Before plucking a flower
For who you are plucking
the flower
That person will love it?

Have you ever think
Before leaving the house
For who you are leaving
Everything
That person will be happy
with you?

Have you ever think
Before make yourself beautiful
That person will notice it?

Sparkling light

I was looking for you
In the blue sky
Where all the stars
Had been sparkling
In the evening

I was looking for you
In my room at the noon
When I was alone
You were not there
But your memories

I was looking for you
When I was playing guitar
You were nowhere
But in the tune

When I found you
I could not stare at you
There was no one
But you and me
I was blushing
And you were smiling
Seeing me blushing

Seeing you smiling
I felt like disappearing
Inside the sparkling stars
Holding you tight
Where no one could see us
But the sparkling light

Never Regret

Have you ever
Put your feet inside
the green grass to
listen to the music
Of nature?

Have you ever
Looked at the open sky
To know the power of God?

Have you ever tried to
Feel music from the breeze
When they are around you
To give you the touch of God?

Everything we have in this
Universe made by you dear God
The nature, the Music, the breeze
And us

Oh God you are everywhere,
you are great
That's why we enjoy our living here
And never regret

The Rain

It is raining
Don't want to
Save me wetting,
I am under the
Cloudy sky
Wanted to walk
Endlessly

Sometime life is
Way more beautiful
You just need to know
How to make it cool…

Making You Fool

Hello rainbow
How are you?
Do you know me?
I know you.
I know you
Since my
Childhood.
When I am sad,
You make my
Mood good.
Love to see you,
When you are
In the blue sky,
Sometime I want
To touch you,
Flying like a
Butterfly.
Want to borrow
Your color,
To make
The world
More beautiful.
Don't want to
Return making
you fool.

The Rain

It's been raining,
Cats and dogs,
Since morning.
My heart is beating,
Seeing you smiling,
Calling me for a walk
Under the moonlight.
The wild breeze
Making me mad.
The sweet tone
Of a nightingale,
Make the moment,
Even more better.
Holding your hand
The thunder
Is roaring,
Making me scared,
Holding you tight.
Sometimes he is you,
Sometimes my dream man.
Kissing me
on my forehead.
With all your love,
The world is quiet.
It's been raining,
Cats and dogs,
Since morning

It's You

What's on my mind?
Nothing but God.
Who send me here,
Living a life
Here and there
When I wake up
In the morning,
First I thank him.
For giving me
One more
Day to live.
Telling me
Oh Sylvie
You are so lucky,
Let's enjoy
The day
With honesty
And dignity
When I wake up
In the morning,
What's on my mind?
Nothing but you
My most powerful God.

The Singing Birds

Think you and I,
Sitting on the top,
Of a huge mountain.
Enjoying the blue sky.
The sun is shining,
And the white clouds
Are playing
touching us,
Getting us wet.
The shiny sun shine,
Helping us to be dry.
The little birds are,
Flying here and there,
Singing the beautiful songs.
Sometimes staying
On our shoulders,
Sometimes
On our hands
Talking to us
Telling us
How happy
They are..
Seeing us enjoying
The nature…
Listening to their songs.

Prophet Moses

Once prophet Moses
Was asking God,
Moses can talk directly
With God whenever
He wish for..
Moses considered
himself lucky.
That's why
He was happy...
God replied Moses back,
You are the lucky one.
But the more lucky,
Is the human.
They just need to pray,
Before they break
Their fasting,
After the day.
I am more close to them,
Listening to their prayer.
For granting their wishes.
Love you my dear Moses.
You Moses my lucky one,
But they are the luckiest

The Moment

It was winter
It was valentine month
The girl was sitting inside the car,
The moment was awesome,
The night was dark.
It was most romantic,
The valentine month
The girl was talking,
Over the phone.
With the boy,
Who she loves the most.
The girl was sitting,
Inside the car.
And was watching
It was snowing
The girl wanted
To hold the moment
The boy who
she was talking,
Was telling her,
With a wet voice.
I love you

I love you
I love you
sweetheart
It was snowing,
It was valentine month.
The boy was saying,
I love you
I love you
My dear
With a deep voice

The girl wanted to
Feel the moment.
It was winter,
It was valentine month.
It was snowing,
The girl was waiting,
For the boy,
With an open heart
It was winter,
It was valentine month

The River

O river o river o river
Do you know
I am in love
O river o river o river
Could you please
Inform my lover
I am waiting here
O river o river o river
Why the wave
Is so beautiful,
Why the breeze
Is so colourful
O river o river o river
Why the nature
Is calling me,
Ask me to stay
Under the blue sky.
Waiting for my lover
Till I die
O river o river o river
Why I Can't stop
Loving you
Because you are my lover
My only dear river

The Cute Little Bird

The cute little bird,
Came to my place,
Hitting herself,
In my glass door.
I was wondering,
And was asking,
Why are you doing this
Dear cute little bird?
Did not get answer,
She ignored me.
And was keep on
Doing that
I was trying to
Convince her,
By giving her food
Bought her a nest,
Failed to convince her
The cute little bird
Sometime some birds,
Want to commit suicide.
May be she was
One of them
My sweet little bird
My heart bleeds,

Remembering her
Even though,
She ignored me,
That cute little bird,
Always remain
In my heart

Honey Needs Money

Today while I was
Planting a plant,
In my garden,
And was talking
To the plant
Asking the plant
With love and care
O dear plant
Could you please
Request God
Make my loved ones
Happy and healthy
Give them money
To help them get honey
My little plant
Starts laughing,
And was asking,
Why are you asking for money?
My dear Sylvie?
I reply back
To my little plant
With joy
If my loved ones have money,

Then they will get honey
My little plant understands,
Give me confirmations,
Will pray to God
To Help my
Loved ones
For getting them
Money for honey

Three Words

"I love you"
These simple
Three words,
Can change your life,
Within a second.
Love is nothing
But good feeling.
It helps you to have a
Good dream,
Good moment.
Sometime
Love bring you
Back old days
Bring you back
Your dream man
Brings you back
Old memories
Love can make
You sing,
Help you fly
Like a butterfly
My love helping me
More writing
More singing
To me love
Is my world
Love to live my life
Inside my world

Wishes

Oh my dear rain
Why are you
So naughty?

Whenever
I try to catch you
You slip
Never allow
Me to hold you
Oh dear clouds
Why are you
So clever?

Whenever
I try to feel you
Standing on top
Of a mountain
You show me
Your presence
Never let me
Hug you

Oh dear rainbow
Why are you
So beautiful??
Whenever
I want to
Make myself
More colourful
Borrowing your colour
You never let me

I run and run and run
Can't find you
Do you really exist?
Oh dear rain bow
Please don't go
Give me your colour
And make me
More beautiful

Hate You

Oh God why
Are you so beautiful?
When I see the nature
I see you
Then can't control tears...

I don't like you
Dear God
You made the world
So gorgeous
And don't let us live here
For ever

I hate you dear God
You give us beautiful heart
There we have endless love
You don't allow us
to love every one
That's not fair to us
Dear God....

Oh my most dearest God
send me to this world
Again and again
If you don't then give me
An opportunities
To love your all creations
till my last breath and
Forever

Red Carpet

Her eyes filled
with tears,
When she saw
The boy was
Holding a red rose
With a killer pose
Standing in a
beautiful garden
To welcome her
With a red carpet

She had no idea
She was so special
to the boy
With whom she was
In deep love

Her heart filled
With joy
Seeing the
Red carpet
And the boy

Seeing the boy
Holding the Rose
With the killer pose

The girl wanted to fly
In the blue sky
Holding the boy
With infinite joy

Hope

It was raining
cats and dogs
Sitting in the porch
A little girl
was enjoying
The noise
of frogs

After the raining
She saw the
Rainbow was dancing

She wanted to join
the dancing rainbow
To make a show

But no luck
The rainbow
was far away
For that
The little girl
had nothing
To say

She was crying
Seeing her crying
Her mother was

Saying don't get
Upset my baby

Hope the next day
The rainbow
Would not be far away
I promise you
My most dearest
Little lady

Love

It is you
Who made me
love you

Who brought me
My dream back?
It is no one
But you

It is you
Who made
Me brave
To enjoy the
world alone
With craze

It is you
Who made me
Hate you
Love and hate
Live together
We just need to be
Careful to avoid the
Second one

It is you
Who made me
Love you

The Gorgeous World

Once in the
nice evening
I was dreaming.

I was laying
on the wave
of a beautiful
Blue ocean......

I was enjoying
the sparkling stars
and the clouds.
The stars and the clouds
were smiling at me
with love and care.

I saw the clouds
Moving here and there.
I was talking to
the clouds
then requesting the clouds
to join me for having fun.
The clouds started laughing

Then said oh dear lady
If I join then you will get wet.

After that you will get sick.
Let me enjoy flying here
and there please

Want to enjoy
seeing you laying
On the wave of
the blue ocean.

Then I replied,
Oh dear cloud
Don't you see I am
Already wet laying
On the wave....?

I just want you to
join me with your
Dazzling presence.

Listening to me
The clouds again said,
Let me enjoy the world
staying in the blue sky

The clouds kept on saying
with a smiling face,
I will definitely join you
To make you happy
Oh dear lady....

The clouds again
kept on saying

I will join you
to make the world more
Beautiful and gorgeous.

Seeing the gorgeous
world you will be happy
my most dearest lady

A Journey By Train

Hi beautiful
I have a dream,
I want to have
A train journey with you,
If you join me,
Please don't say no to me

I will show
You mountain,
From inside the train,
There will be
No one but
You and me
Oh dear lady,
Want to have a
Journey with you,
If you join me,
Please don't say no to me

I will show you river,
When we will
be together,
Holding each other,
No matter what,
Oh baby please
join me,
Want to have a

Journey with you,
Please don't say no to me

Hi beautiful
I have a dream,
Want to have a journey
With you,
Please don't say no to me

Blinking

One blinking
takes a year,
Few blinking
Takes a lifetime.

Time is running
Like a speedy horse,
That's why scared
Of aging
Trying to hold
It tight

Want to enjoy life
Till my last breath
It might be today
or tomorrow
Because life is not
Endless

Make Your Life Better

If you see
Your dream is on the
Other side of the clouds,
Make your reach long,
Move the clouds,
Grab your dream,
Make your life better

If you feel
Your time will finish,
Don't be scared,
Move out,
Stay under the blue sky,
Take a deep breath,
Start fresh

If you see
Your life is ruined,
Don't worry,
There is nothing to be regret,
Don't look back,
Step forward

If you feel
No one loves you,
Don't be sad,
There is nothing to be upset,
Spread love,
Feel better

Little Squirrel

It was evening
Of a summer
month of Ramadan.
I was fasting then
Felt like walking.

The time was evening
And the sun was setting,
The nature was reddish,
I was walking alone
In the street.

While walking alone
In the beautiful street
I saw a naughty squirrel
Enjoying the nature
Jumping here and there
Inside a beautiful garden

Seeing the squirrel jumping
I was staring then felt like
I am in heaven
I tried to say hello
To that cute squirrel

The squirrel was busy
Even so looked at me,

Replied me back saying hello
With a cute smile
No one understood but me

It was a heavenly feeling
I will never forget
Then I came back home
Informed my family
About my sweet memory
How I met the squirrel
While walking alone
In the beautiful street.

I described my family
How I met a cute squirrel
How I greeted the squirrel
How the Squirrel smiled
at me then wished me hello.

It was a beautiful moment
I was sharing my memory
with my lovely family
It was a month of Ramadan
I was walking alone in the street
And the time was evening

Silver Light

Oh dear moon
Why did not you come
Last night in my dream
Dear moon

I was waiting for you
Till the morning
But no luck
Dear moon

You spread the silver light
In the night in my dream
I caught your light
Staying under the
Open sky
To make me beautiful
Dear moon

Oh dear moon
Why you did not come
Last night in my dream
I was waiting for you
Till the morning
But no luck
Dear moon

Black

Knock, knock
I asked,
Who is it?
It's me color black,
Color black replied.
Then requested
Please open the door.

I asked,
What do you want
Color black?
Color black replied,
Nothing but love.....

I asked
Why are you sad
My dear color black?
She replied,
I am black
That's why
I am sad.

I opened the door,
Welcomed her,
I hugged her,
Then told her,
Don't get upset
My dear black.....

I kept on saying
If you would not exist
How the color white
Would get importance?

If the evening would
Not be black,
How would we enjoy
The sunny morning?

If the night would not be dark
How would we enjoy
the beautiful moon?
And the sparkling stars
In the open sky?

I kept on saying
To make color black happy,
Can't you see?
When our loving one die
We wear black dress
To show respect?
Can't you see
We wear black dress
To impress our boyfriends
When we are on date

Don't you know?
You hold all the colors,
In your body
That's why all the colors
Are happy staying in
your body

Listening to my words
Color black became happy
Gave me a tight hug
Then said good bye
to fly in the blue sky

Wondering

When I will be lost
Will you stop
searching for me?
It can't be

When I will be far away
Will you stop hold me
open your arms?
It can't be

When I will be sick
Enjoying the rain
Under the open sky
Will you stop me from
Enjoying the nature?
It can't be

When I will be
Scared seeing the
Huge wave of the ocean
Will you stop me staying
Near the sea shore
It can't be

When you see
I might get hurt
Loving you

Will you stop me
Loving you?
It can't be

Open your eyes
If you get nothing
Forget everything
Overcome all your pain
If I am lost
Forever
It can be

They Met In A Crowded Place (Part I)

They met in a
crowed place,
But did not talk much
When they met at first

It happened in the
Evening of a
Beautiful winter
As a witness
I was there

They exchanged
Phone numbers.
After they talked
They found somehow
their thoughts
Had been similar

It was a love story
I want to describe you
Through a poetry

They had to meet secretly
Because they fell in love madly
They were teenagers
That's why they could not
Avoid each other

From the very beginning
The girl wanted
to be a friend,
But the boy did not
Let it happen

He killed the girl with
His daring actions,

Also with some
Bold words

Then the girl fell in love
With the romantic
Bold words
Of that darling boy.

One day the boy said
To that bubbly girl,
"I want to go with you
By a beautiful lake.
Want to hold your
hands there
Kissing your forehead
Want to love your eyes
Touch my lips"

The teenage girl could
not control herself,
Said yes to the daring boy
Right that moment.
Also became crazy for
The darling boy
Wanted to meet him
Every day by the lake
in her dream.

They met, they walked
Holding hands of each other
Then they kissed...

I cannot describe anymore
Because I enjoyed
the love story in my dream.

My dearest readers I am
Really very sorry,
Will inform you the next
Love scene very soon writing
One more beautiful poetry

They Met In A Crowded Place (Part II)

One day the teens
were talking over
the phone.
Had been discussing
How they want to meet
holding hands of
each other, closing
their eyes.

The teen girl described to the boy
How she wanted to meet him.

She wanted to meet the boy
beside a sea shore,
when the sun will be setting.
She also said the boy should
be there holding a red rose

When they will meet
No one will be talking
There will be only infinite
silence, without blinking
The girl will be keep on smiling
holding the red rose under
the beautiful sun setting.

What the boy will do?
The boy will also keep
on walking without talking
What about the teen girl?
She will be enjoying the silence
of the boy with joy.

Then they both will hold
The hands touching
Their small fingers
With love and joy.

What will happen next?
I don't want to describe
the poetry anymore.
Because they both will be
diving in the blue ocean
to be lost there forever.

Cinderella

Once a little girl was
Requesting her dad
"Dad will you please
Divorce my mummy?"

Dad was wondering,
Asked the little girl back,
"Why do you want me to
Divorce your mummy??"

The little girl replied
"You can bring
Me a step mummy then".

Dad started enjoying
With the reply of his
Little princess
He asked her back
"If I will bring you a step mom
she will torture you then"

The little girl answered
"I want to be tortured by
My step mom. Please dad
Bring me two step sisters as well"

Dad started laughing
Hugging his daughter, he asked
"Why do you want me to bring
you step mom with step sisters??"

The little girl made her eyes big
Then she was describing her dad
with a very strong tone
"Look dad, if you bring me a step mom
with step sisters,
I will become Cinderella then,
A prince will come,
Riding in a carriage,
Will marry me then,
With the help of a fairy Godmother
I want to be Cinderella dad
Help me please"

Dad laughed a lot
Held his little princess
In his arms then confirmed her
"No matter what
I will make your dreams come true
You are my Cinderella
One day a prince will come
Riding in a carriage
Will marry you and
Give you a glass shoe"

With the reply of her dad
The little girl relaxed

Then fell asleep in her dads arms
Before sleeping she was thinking
"I don't have to have a step mom
to become Cinderella
as long as my dad is with me........"

Roman Holiday

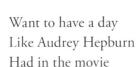

Want to have a day
Like Audrey Hepburn
Had in the movie
Roman holiday

There will be no
Responsibilities and
I will forget everything

Will be laying under the
Beautiful cloudy sky
Will be floating in the
Waves of a roaring sea
Feeling like opening the
Door to heaven
With a golden key

Then my hero will come
Riding in a Vespa
Like Gregory Peck
The movie star
He will request me to
Run away with him
To be lost forever
With infinite love

If I will be a tune
You will be a flute then

If you will be an open sky
I will be a sparkling star then

If you will be the darling moon
I will keep on shining then

If you will be the morning
I will keep on lighting then

If you will be the dark evening
I will keep on crying then

May Be

We all are tied with the rules
Of manmade society
Don't have courage to break it

If I will break the rules of
So called manmade systems
Then the society will consider
Me a bad girl

What is society giving me?
Nothing but tons of rules

Aging brings me feelings
Of emptiness
Want to experience a crazy life

Good girl, loving wife, caring mother
Tired of hearing
All these meaningless words

I am frustrated, I am lost
Want to be naughty, want to be crazy
Want to break the barricade
Of all the bullshit systems

Want to fly under the open sky
May be alone may be not

The Roots

It was monsoon
The newlywed couple
Enjoying the rain,
On their honeymoon
In a village

The village
Full of natural beauty,
The soil of that village,
Bringing them the fragrance
Of ESTEE LAUDER beyond paradise.

The hut they were living in,
Was giving them the comfort
Of a five star resort
The rain was sounding like
The concert of
Western classical Music Beethoven.

The food was
Tasting like it was Cooked by Iron chef
Both of them were nature lovers,
Also rich enough.
Did not go to Switzerland
To enjoy their honeymoon!
Was crying holding each other,
For their love of the roots

Don't Let It Go

Smile with everyone
Even when your
Heart is Bleeding

Don't let the world
Pity you when you are crying.
Build your heart strong
Don't let anybody know that.

Don't show your heart is soft inside.
Don't let your fake friends
Wipe your tears,
Don't let anybody know
What your fears.

Live your life with elegance.
Make yourself more intelligent.
Live your life to the fullest.
Show everyone that
You are the coolest.

Life is short we all know
So enjoy each and
Every moment
Please don't let it go.

The Last Departure

Last departure means not to be lost
To eternity
Last departure means
A great freedom
To the eternity

Last departure is not only
Shedding tears,
It means accepting
The eternity
With love and care.

Don't torture
present life
For preparing
last departure.
To me last departure
Is a bridge in between
Life and heaven.

I consider last departure
A sweet return
With dignity and grace.

I consider last Departure as a
Great return to
The lord who made us
For a beautiful purpose.

Last departure
Might be a sweet
Return to the eternity,
Leaving some heart
Touching poetries,
Stories, music or a
Great painting.

Last departure could be a
Beautiful smile
With a loving look
Just before we lost
To eternity

Can't Call It Illicit

Love is God's gift
We should not
Call it illicit

It comes without
Knowing
Like a wild wind

Sometime like a
Thunder
To burn everything

The Birds Are Happy

Think you and I
Sitting on the top
Of a huge mountain
For enjoying the blue sky

The sun is shining,
The white clouds
Are playing here and there,
Pouring on us as a rain
For making us wet

The shiny sun shine
Helping us to be dry.
The little birds are
Flying in the open sky
Singing the beautiful songs

Sometimes they staying
On our shoulders,
Some times on our hands
Whispering to us
For informing us
How happy they are
Seeing us enjoying
The nature
Listening to their
Music together

It's My Time

It's my time,
I don't have to do anything,
Enjoying me-time
with my iPad,
From 8pm to midnight,
It's only my time

It's my time,
I don't have to do anything,
Writing in my iPad,
Whatever I want to,
It's only my time

It's my time,
I don't have to do anything,
Watching movies on Netflix,
Narcos or Cinderella,
Whatever I like to,
It's only my time

It's my time,
I don't have to do anything

Dreaming of Che Guevara,
Or Shukanto,
Whoever I like to,
It's only my time

It's my time,
Whatever I like to do,
That's my right,
Because it is only my time

Fall

Oh fall, Oh fall,
When you come,
You bring us color
You bring us beauty
You remind us
Of teenage,
My darling fall.

Oh dear fall,
You are as beautiful
As a teenaged girl.
Teenage beauty
Never last long,
Just like you
My dear fall

Oh fall, oh fall
Why do you
Remind me old age?
Don't you know?
When you go,

The nature
Looks helpless
Just like them,
Who turn
Into old age.
My dear fall.

Oh dear fall,
Please Don't go,
Stay forever,
Never say
Goodbye
Make me again
Evergreen,
Just like a
Beautiful teen

Printed in the United States
By Bookmasters